# Anger Management

## A Simple Guide To Achieving Calmness And Getting Rid Of Anger From Your Life For Good!

# Table of Contents

(This page is intentionally left blank)

# Why You Need To Read This Book

Do you feel like you're a ticking time bomb waiting to go off?

Do you feel like you just can't seem to control your anger even when you try to?

Do people tell you you're always angry but you're not really sure why?

What about when you lose control and hurt the people you love?

It's so frustrating right!

Especially when you don't want to be like that!

If you answer yes to any of these questions, then this book will help you discover how to achieve calmness and get rid of anger from your life completely.

Even if you thought it is impossible.

In this book you'll discover:

- Where you anger comes from
- What type of anger you have
- How to get over your past events that cause you pain

- How to calm your angry urges
- How to make head-way towards calmness
- How to manage and control your anger for good

# Chapter 1: About Your Anger

Anger is a self-defense mechanism that we need to learn to control.

Parents, teachers and other adults in our life are supposed to help us understand anger and thus how to control it.

When anger management issues arise in adults, it may mean you have never received a good example of how to explore your anger, the root of it or learned how to control it.

If your anger becomes rage, where you are hurting yourself or others, it is time to discover the underlying cause.

## What is the Root of Your Anger?

Discovering the root of your anger may take time.

It will require self-reflection. Anger can arise from known and hidden factors.

Known factors are often what happens that make it easy for you to justify your anger.

For example, while driving a person may cut you off or drive erratically and cause your anger.

With hidden anger it is harder to discover the root cause.

It may be linked to the following concepts, in terms of how it will manifest itself.

- Procrastination

- Habitual lateness

- Sarcasm

- Frequent sighing

- Smiling even though you are hurting

- Frequent disturbed sleep and dreams

- Excessive irritability over trivial things

- Facial tics

Anger, when hidden, usually comes from a place that is more difficult to assess because it can go back to childhood, numerous incidents of bullying that we may even have forgotten about, or be more relevant to the present.

Linking anger to a root cause usually comes down to one emotion—happiness—where you do not feel happy no matter what happens in your life.

You may feel cursed, vilified, or constantly used, which leads to unhappiness.

Fear, pain, and frustration are leading causes of anger and may be why you feel unhappy.

To figure out the root of your anger, you will need to use self-reflection.

Before moving on to self-reflection, there is one caveat to the root of your anger that may not be linked to happiness.

Health troubles are a cause of anger.

Thyroid disease, which is linked to hormones, can cause depression, anger, confusion, distrust, anxiety, and physical discomfort.

Your anger and how you manage it, if linked to an underlying medical condition, may not improve until the medical issue is corrected.

If you know you do not have a medical condition that would affect the production of hormones that interfere with your emotions, then you can safely start looking at why you are angry instead of happy.

## Assessing Your Anger - Importance of Self-Reflection

Why are you angry?

Has anyone ever asked you the question?

Perhaps your child, a friend, or your spouse has asked, "Why are you always angry?"

But you are unable to provide an answer.

It is the question that will get everything in this section started.

You need to ask yourself why you are angry all the time.

What is it about your life or your situation that makes you quickly resort to anger?

There are external and internal factors that affect us.

An external factor is not something we can control all the time.

For instance, you may be going through a divorce.

The other person may not be following the divorce decree or parenting plan (if you have children) and that may lead to anger.

A person who has been emotionally abused may be quick to feel anger when control continues to slip from their fingers, despite feeling they are free from the abuse.

External anger typically relates to another person and, in some cases, it is warranted, but there are ways to manage it.

You do not have to let your anger rise due to external factors especially when they relate to feeling a loss of control in your life.

It is better to find ways to feel in control of the parts of your life if you can and remember to let go of the things you are unable to control.

Internal factors for rage usually stem from childhood and not being taught how to handle anger.

It may be that your parent or parents had the same actions, and you picked them up thinking your anger was natural and correct.

However, it may also come from a type of anger you have, such as a passive feeling that makes you passively angry.

Self-reflection is important for you to assess your anger.

Until you know the root cause or causes, as there may be more than one, you are not going to be able to move forward.

## Suggested Action Task - Self Analysis

When you ask, "Why are you angry," face the question head on and with honesty.

Figure out whether fear, pain or frustration is hiding underneath the anger you readily adopted.

It is time for you to follow through with what you have learned.

The following suggestions are meant to help you face your anger, find it, and figure out how to deal with it.

1. Get a piece of paper, open a word processor, or use a journal.

2. Try writing your current emotions. If you are feeling angry, this is the time when you need to face it.

3. Find the root cause of this anger. Are you afraid of job loss, feeling emotionally abused, fear of failure, fear that you are causing harm to others? List all the causes you believe may be behind your current feelings.

4. Figure out how to deal with the fear, pain, and/or frustration. Whether another person is providing the pain, or it is physical find a solution. If you are fearful talk with someone or write about why you feel this fear. Frustration can build up or be happening right now—write about these moments—you will discover a way to get rid of the frustration.

5. You can choose how you respond. You get to choose to think about the positive and let go of the negative.

Your journal is the way to find the patterns in your behavior and continue to self-reflect to discover the root causes in any given situation.

# Chapter 2: Understanding Types of Anger

Knowing the root of your anger and reflecting on it, is a positive start to managing your anger better; however, you still have a few steps to do before you have a solid plan.

One step is to understand the types of anger and identify which one or ones you feel during incidents of high anger and rage.

## Passive Anger

Passive anger can be combined with aggressive anger in a passive-aggressive situation.

The passive type of anger is where you do not confront the problem but evade such an experience.

You feel fury and irritation; however, you remain silent.

You might use sarcasm, silence or mockery.

You tend not to use actions that would be aggressive.

However, while you do not perceive them as aggressive the receiver may.

For example, a veiled statement or sarcasm is overly aggressive, even when stated in a passive way.

You are not being physical, but you can be harming another person with your temper on an emotional level.

## Aggressive Anger

Aggressive anger or behavioral anger as some psychologists may refer to it is when you lash out at the object causing your anger.

You feel overwhelmed and unable to keep your emotions on an even keel.

Typically, aggressive anger leads to breaking things, throwing items, or hurting another person.

It is unpredictable and can lead to legal action, as well as interpersonal troubles.

## Self-inflicted Anger

It can also be considered self-abusive anger because a person inflicting anger on themselves is often harming their self.

Self-abusive anger comes from a shame-based situation.

You tend to feel unworthy, ashamed, humiliated, or hopeless.

You internalize these feelings until you are in a situation of negative reactions.

You may talk to yourself, mentally, where you are mean and negative about your attributes.

You may harm yourself physically by using alcohol, substances, eating incorrectly, or physically cut yourself.

Self-inflicted anger does not have to become abusive.

However, in the majority of people it will in some way manifest itself in a physical expression of pain.

Self-inflicted anger is going to derive from shame, emotional abuse, and doubt, where you do not think you are worthy of care from another or to even go on living.

## Habitual Anger

Habitual or chronic anger is an ongoing resentment.

You will resent others in your life, feel frustration in specific situations, or feel angry at yourself.

Habitual anger is something you fall into quickly and forget that it can lead to adverse troubles, not only for your wellbeing, but also for your health.

The resentment or frustration causes you to act out, to avoid paying attention to your health, and forget there may be a real cause within you versus an external cause for your anger.

## Paranoid Anger

Paranoid anger does not need to link to a more serious psychological disorder, such as a personality disorder.

However, in some situations it does.

Paranoia can link to psychotic disorders where there are delusions or feelings of paranoia that someone is attempting to harm you when there is no external force for such harm.

Schizophrenia, dementia, thyroid hormone issues, personality disorders, and bipolar disorder are typically linked to paranoid anger.

A person who is paranoid will feel anxious with thoughts of persecution, conspiracy or threat.

You may believe another person is out to mistreat you or do you harm, so you feel mistrust, defensive, hypervigilant and cannot think of forgiving another for their transgressions.

You tend to be preoccupied with hidden fear, motives, and being deceived.

You can also project your feelings onto others, stating they are doing things to you, when you are actually being self-inflicting and abusive.

## Trauma Anger

Traumatic anger has several root causes.

The leading example is PTSD or post traumatic stress disorder.

PTSD arises from being in a very troubling situation.

Coming back from war, being a police officer in high-stress situations or being a hostage can be reasons to develop PTSD.

Anyone involved in 9-11 or mass shootings can also suffer from PTSD.

Emotional abuse during childhood or in adulthood, physically abusive relationships and other trauma related scenarios can all lead to heightened anger.

Anger is common in a person suffering from a trauma because it helps them to feel alive.

Your adrenaline kicks up with anger, allowing you to feel like you survived and are living.

Anger is also part of the healing process, where you may ask "why me" or "why not me?"

For instance, a person who survived a roadside bombing while the rest of the men and women did not may feel angry at surviving.

Anger is a sign of healing, processing, but it still needs to be dealt with and managed.

## Suggested Action Task - Identify Your Anger

It is plausible for a person to have more than one type of anger, given the situations they may find themselves in, and that is why you should work to identify the types of anger you have.

1. Try going back to your journal and looking at the root cause?

   Did you find one for your current anger or your existing anger?

2. If not, take time to self-reflect and determine how often your anger presents itself.

   Do you feel anger daily?

   Are there certain situations or people who cause your anger to increase?

   Write these down in your journal to keep a record.

3. Use your journal every time you feel anger or rage.

   Where were you?

   Who was around you?

   What incited your anger?

   How do you think you could have reacted better?

4. Examine the list of anger types.

   Which explanation best fits your current feelings?

   Do you feel your anger is extremely common?

   Do you have a trauma associated with your anger?

Make a record each time you feel anger and see if you can identify the same type of anger each time.

You can feel diverse types of anger.

You may have a prevalence for one type, which is going to help to control your rage.

# Chapter 3: How To Control & Manage Your Anger

Congratulations, you have reached the point where you can learn how to control and manage your anger.

There are four topics to explore before we turn to some helpful actions that have been highly effective for anyone who needs to learn how to control and manage their anger.

## Getting Over Your Past Events

Past events are an area that must be faced before you can move on and manage your anger.

It is an easy statement to write, but not something simple to change.

Whether incidents happen in childhood or adulthood, they shape us and how we are going to react.

When we are faced with the past events on a daily basis, it is even more difficult to get over the issues.

Let's go back to the divorce situation, mentioned in section one.

What if you were emotionally abused during your nearly two-decade marriage?

What if you thought, "I'm free" only to find the person creating the emotional abuse is still attempting to control you?

In this real situation, the former marriage partner is narcissistic with borderline personality disorder.

The person who feels depressed and is easy to anger uses sarcasm to deflect and blames the other person for all issues.

Due to children being involved, communication has to remain between the two parties, where the former marriage partner attempts to control everything and belittle their ex.

In this situation, how do you let go of past events, when the force causing the anger is still present?

One of the best things learned from situations regarding the past is the statement "I will let go of the things or people I cannot control and focus on what I can control."

You cannot control another person, your past, or certain situations, dwelling on this loss of control will more than likely lead to continued anger.

It is better to focus on the elements of your life that you can control.

Repeating the quoted statement is one way for you to take a deep breath, focus, and tell your mind to focus on what is possible.

## How to Calm Your Angry Urges

Psychologists, psychotherapists, psychiatrists, doctors and various other mental health and health professionals tell most people to use a journal at the beginning of anger management.

For some individuals, journal writing is not the way; particularly, if you do not like writing.

However, the steps you would use in a journal can apply.

1. Write the incident down when you felt anger.

2. How did you react?

3.  What are five ways you could have reacted better?

When you can remember the incident, reflect on your reaction and find an alternative or better methods to react, you can come to terms with a way to calm your anger.

At first you may not be able to discover a better reaction, especially, in the moment.

When you calm down, you will want to self-reflect.

Eventually, you are going to reach a point where you can use calming techniques during your anger phase.

Here are some suggestions for calming your anger during or after an incident.

- Count to five or keeping counting if you need to.

- Take a deep breath, repeat until you feel your nerves are calming down.

- Think of a happy memory. It can be from childhood or a more recent memory. For one person, thinking about being in a swimming pool, counting lap after lap, is calming. It is even better to be swimming.

- Exercise, such as running or lifting weights. The exercise should be solitary, where you are alone with your thoughts. Exercise is a fantastic way to help you meditate, where you let your mind empty and only think about your feet moving you forward. You do not want basketball or other activities that would involve other people as this can lead to more anger.

- Take a bath. Like swimming or running, a bath can be a place where you relax. The ambiance with or without music, candles, or no lights, can help you calm your mind and body.

- Meditation is another way to reach a state of calm. During meditation, you are to let thoughts come and go, never dwelling on anything in particular. In fact, if a thought comes into your mind that makes you angry, you physically shove it out the door of your mind and replace it with a happier thought. You can also make a statement in your mind "I will not think about that until I am calm and ready."

## Positive Self-talk

Self-talk or self-writing are two ways for you to reach a better image of yourself.

Anger can derive from shame, feelings of unworthiness, depression, jealousy, and other negative emotions.

By correcting how your mind talks about you, and only you can do this, you are going to reach a new state of calm and happiness.

1. Choose to write in a journal, talk to yourself in the mirror, or simply repeat positive feedback in your mind.

2. Before you get out of bed, lay there for five minutes.

3. Think of one thing you can say about you that is positive. For example, do you like your hair, your facial structure? Did you get a positive message from your boss or anything else that makes you feel good?

4. Repeat this process each time you feel anger closing in so that you avoid letting the rage take over.

You can also make these statements during the shower, making a meal, or sitting in your favorite chair.

The suggestion of "bed" is made because it is a time when you are either going to sleep or just waking up and being positive before you sleep or get up for the new day, helps you relax and prepare.

Positive self-talk is best when you are in a relaxed state and when you are about to head into an angry feeling.

## How to Make Headway Towards Calmness

The above section about calming angry urges can apply here as a way to start the process.

You also have more options to ensure you have a calmer lifestyle than you may have had to this point.

One of the biggest troubles people who are angry have is looking around and seeing the things they cannot control.

Everywhere they look, the control is out of their hands, so to remain calm - you need to find your control.

It can start small.

When you are overwhelmed, it is always a better idea to find one small thing that helps you feel in control.

The mundane tasks of life are ways to let this happen. Here are some suggestions.

- Clean an area of your home. Once that area is complete, how do you feel? You should feel accomplished. You may feel you have completed one task. Many who use cleaning to remove anger will feel calm and more in control because they have managed one task that needed completing.

- Confront your anger, even if it is only in your mind. For example, if it is a person who consistently makes you angry, what can you say to that person? If you imagine the conversation you should have to let them know their behavior hurts you, then you can begin to use those words when you are faced with this person.

- Avoidance is a healthy way of gaining calm in angry situations, as long as you return to the reason for your anger when you have reached a better frame of mind. For instance, you might think, "I will not deal with these emotions now, tomorrow is another day." Yes, the last part is a great line from an immensely popular Civil War fiction. Tomorrow is another day, and sometimes letting yourself cool down, spending time on your own, and positive thinking to yourself about your best qualities, helps you face the anger of the past.

## Suggested Action Task - Change for Good

You have learned a lot about anger and controlling those feelings of rage.

Here are some last tips to help you.

1. Tell yourself, repeatedly if necessary, it is going to take time for you to learn how to control your anger. Setbacks will occur.

2. Sometimes anger is healthy, you will learn how to differentiate these times, once you work on your past and the types of anger you feel.

3. Change your mindset, and you will change how you control your mind. You are the keeper of your brain, and how it acts. Until you see yourself in a positive light, the world around you will continue to anger you.

4. Use a journal, self-talk, or similar methods each day, to help boost your confidence. Work each day on how to be more positive.

5. Seek help if you discover you need an extra hand. Asking for help from a professional in anger management does not mean you are wrong or ill. It means you understand your anger is hurting your relationships and you are unable to completely change without a helping hand.